AF584806

AUSTRALIA'S REMARKABLE WILDLIFE

JOHN LESLEY

WALLABY

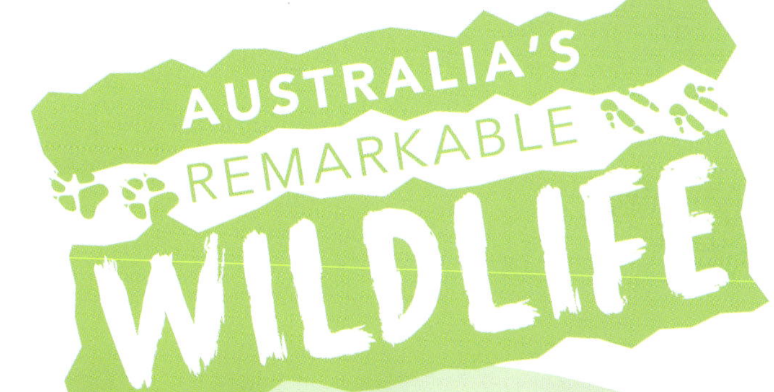

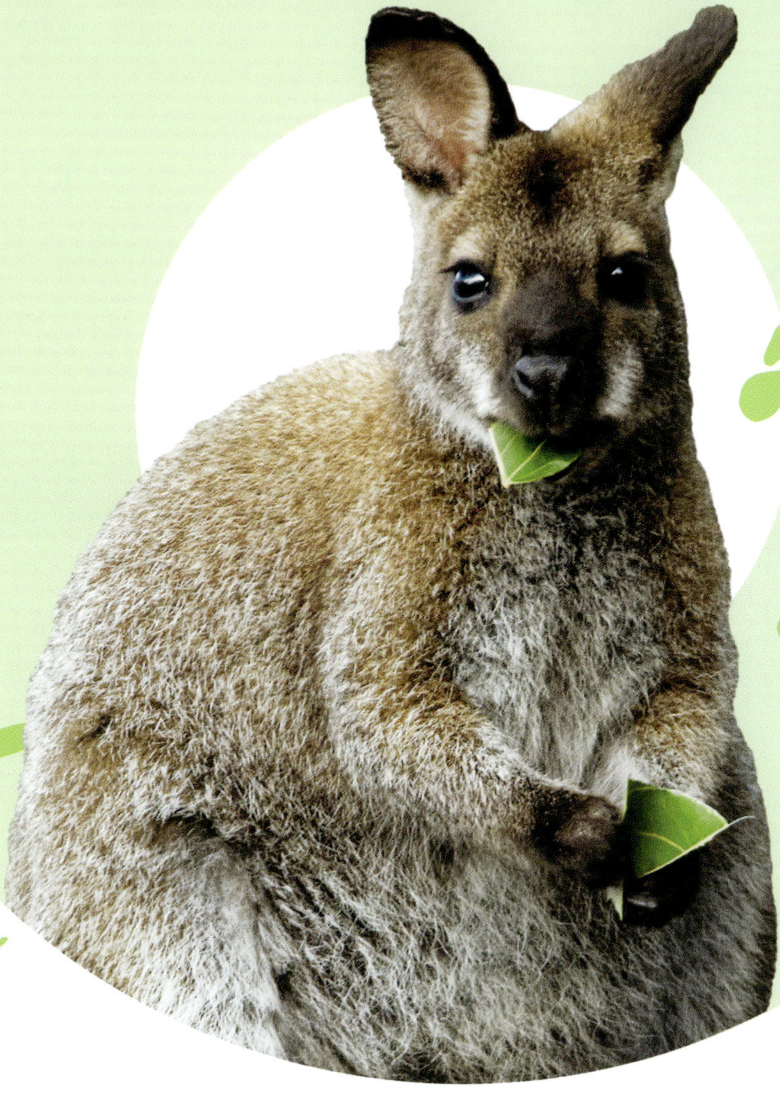

REDBACK publishing

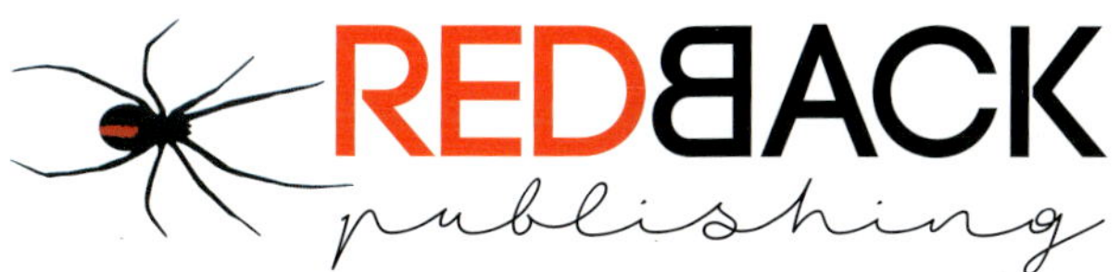

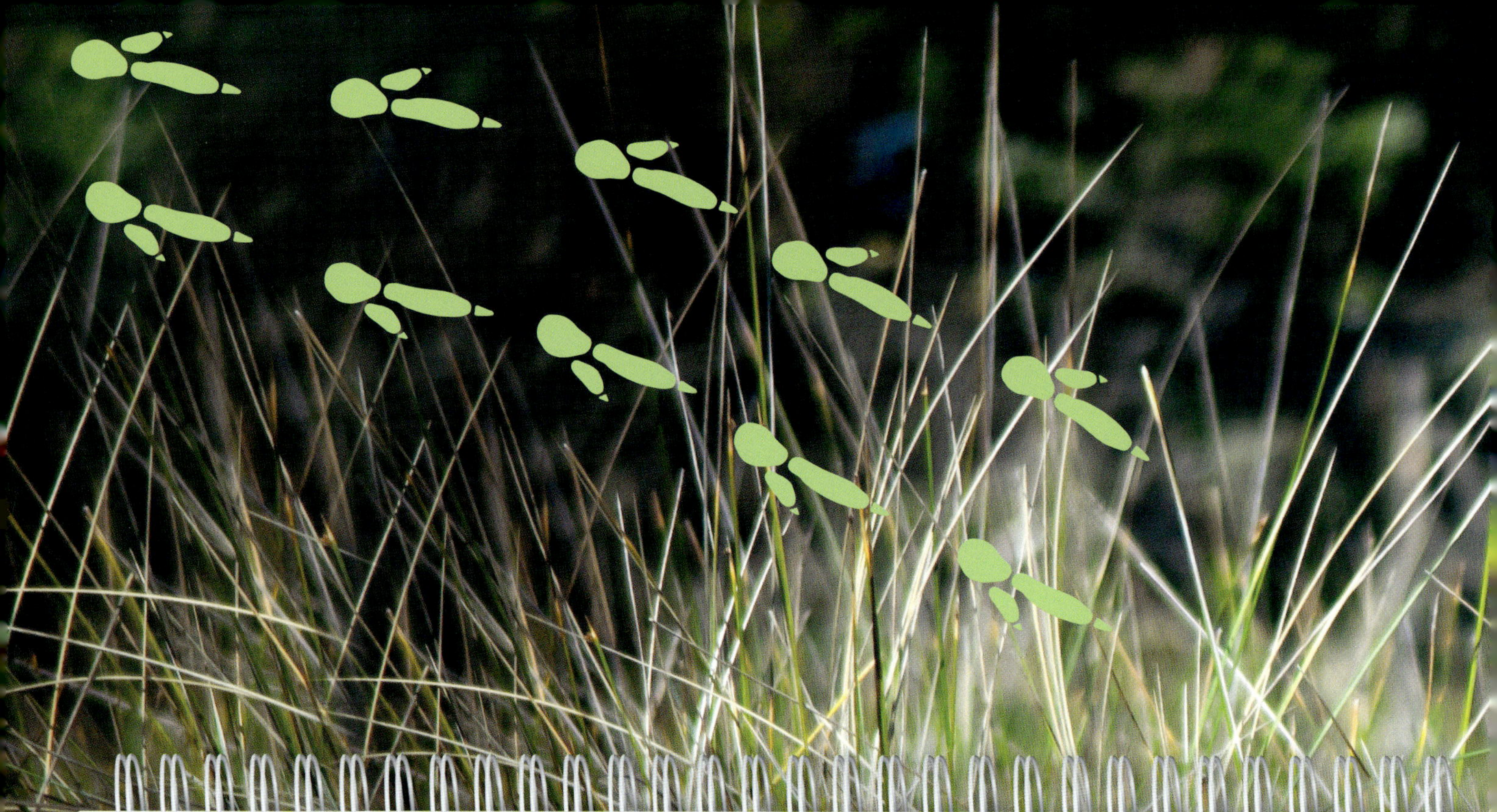

First Published 2024 by
Redback Publishing
Suite 6, 13a Narabang Way,
Belrose NSW 2085
Australia

www.redbackpublishing.com
info@redbackpublishing.com

ISBN 978-1-761400-68-1

Author: John Lesley
Editor: Caroline Thomas
Design: Redback Publishing

A catalogue record for this book is available from the National Library of Australia

Originated by Redback Publishing

Acknowledgements
Abbreviations: l—left, r—right, b—bottom, t—top, c—centre, m—middle
We would like to thank the following for permission to reproduce photographs: (Images © shutterstock)
p15 Ian Beattie © Alamy; p22tr Nobu Tamura (http://spinops.blogspot.com), CC BY 3.0 <https://creativecommons.org/licenses/by/3.0>, via Wikimedia Commons; p23tr Nobu Tamura (http://spinops.blogspot.com), CC BY 3.0 <https://creativecommons.org/licenses/by/3.0>, via Wikimedia Commons; p23bl Charles-Alexandre Lesueur, Public domain, via Wikimedia Commons; p27tr Joseph Lycett, Public domain, via Wikimedia Commons; p30tl DiverDave, CC BY-SA 3.0 <https://creativecommons.org/licenses/by-sa/3.0>, via Wikimedia Commons; p31mr State of Queensland, CC BY 4.0 <https://creativecommons.org/licenses/by/4.0>, via Wikimedia Commons

CONTENTS

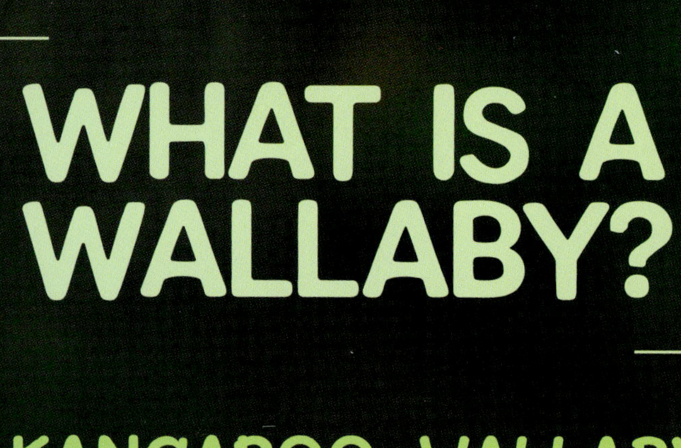

WHAT IS A WALLABY?

KANGAROO, WALLABY OR WALLAROO?

People often group all these animals together as kangaroos. They are all in the marsupial animal group called macropods, but they are actually all very different from each other.

KANGAROOS

The four largest species of kangaroo are in a group by themselves, and include red kangaroos, eastern and western grey kangaroos, and antilopine kangaroos.

WALLAROOS

A wallaroo is neither a wallaby nor a kangaroo. It is midway between the two. Some people call the antilopine kangaroo *(Macropus antilopinus)* a wallaroo.

Wallaroo

WALLABIES

Wallabies are smaller than kangaroos. There are many species of wallaby and they have a vast range of habitats across Australia, from deserts to dense forests. People sometimes use the term 'wallaby' to refer to any small macropod, such as a quokka or pademelon.

Quokka

OTHER MACROPODS

At the smaller end of the size range of marsupial macropods are the rat-kangaroos, bettongs, quokkas, pademelons and potoroos.

MACROPODS

Macropod is the group name for kangaroos, wallabies and wallaroos. Quokkas, bettongs, potoroos and pademelons are also included. The word 'macropod' means large foot.

Macropods are native to Australia and New Guinea.

Most macropods have large back legs and feet, and a heavy, long tail that they use for balance. They hop rather than walk, although the tree kangaroos can also climb trees.

Tree kangaroo

Main image: Western brush wallaby

MARSUPIALS

All macropods are marsupials. The characteristics of a marsupial are:

- They give birth to tiny, underdeveloped babies
- The young drink milk from their mother who keeps them in a pouch or a fold of her skin

WALLABY BASIC FACTS

All wallabies are macropods, marsupials and mammals.

SIZE & SHAPE

The difference between the largest kangaroo macropod and the smallest wallaby is enormous. An adult male red kangaroo can stand well over two metres tall, while the smallest macropods weigh under a kilogram.

TEETH

Wallabies and kangaroos have different types of teeth. Wallabies graze on leaves, grass and fruit in forests and the bush, so they need flat teeth. Kangaroos graze on a lot of grass so they have sharper teeth to cut through it more easily.

LEGS

Red and grey kangaroos have massive back legs in comparison to the rest of their body size. Wallaby legs are not as large in comparison. Wallabies mostly live in forests and rocky areas, so their smaller back legs and hopping movements are more useful adaptations for living in these habitats.

COLOUR

Wallabies tend to have multiple colours of browns and greys in their coat, while kangaroo coats are usually just the one colour, either grey or reddish.

TYPES OF WALLABY

ROCK WALLABY

FACT FILE

Scientific name: Genus *Petrogale*
Colour: Browns, yellows and greys
Size: Weight ranges from one to a few kilograms. Length under a metre
Habitat: Live in steep, rocky areas where they hop from shelf to shelf
Food: They come out from their rocky shelters at night to feed on plants and grasses

Many rock wallaby species are under threat of extinction. They are losing their habitats, they are killed by feral animals, and they live in small groups that interbreed and therefore do not have enough genetic diversity to successfully fight new diseases.

There are many species of rock wallaby, including the yellow-footed rock wallaby, the brush-tailed rock wallaby and the monjon. Rock wallabies are also closely related to tree kangaroos.

SWAMP WALLABY

FACT FILE

Scientific name: *Wallabia bicolor*
Other names: Black wallaby, black-tailed wallaby, stinkers
Colour: Black paws, tail and face, and brown/black fur. The tail tip may be white
Size: Body about 70 centimetres long, plus tail
Habitat: Eastern Australia in dense forests and bushy areas
Food: Grass, leaves and bushes

Swamp wallabies have a swampy smell. New Zealand imported a few swamp wallabies in the 1800s, and they now live there in the wild.

AGILE WALLABY

FACT FILE

Scientific name: *Macropus agilis*
Other name: Sandy wallaby
Colour: Pale, brownish yellow, with a white belly and black edges to the ears
Size: Body 80 centimetres long, plus tail
Habitat: Subtropical grasslands and bush of northern Australia and southern New Guinea
Food: Mostly eat grasses and shrubs, but will sometimes annoy farmers by eating crops

Saltwater crocodiles prey on the agile wallaby, a threat that wallabies in the south of Australia do not have to face. Going to a water hole or creek to drink can be a dangerous activity in the Top End!

REC

4K UHD

3...2...1...1...2...3

00:35:02

PARMA WALLABY

FACT FILE

Scientific name: *Macropus parma*
Other names: White-fronted wallaby, white-throated pademelon
Colour: Grey with a white front
Size: Body about half a metre long, plus tail
Habitat: Forests of eastern Australia
Food: Herbivore

Parma wallabies are very vulnerable to attack by feral predators and to loss of habitat. From a human point of view, parma wallabies are some of the cutest!

RED-NECKED WALLABY

FACT FILE

Scientific name: *Macropus rufogriseus*
Other names: Bennetts wallaby
Colour: Grey and reddish brown, with black paws
Size: About 80 centimetres tall, and weighing up to 20 kilograms
Habitat: Forests and grassy bushland of eastern Australia
Food: Grasses, leaves and plants

A small population of wild, red-necked wallabies lives in Britain, where they were taken over a hundred years ago.

This wallaby is so large that it is often mistaken for a kangaroo. It is not currently under threat of extinction, and it often enters gardens that border on natural bushland.

BLACK-STRIPED WALLABY

Already endangered in New South Wales, the black-striped wallaby suffered during the massive bushfires of 2019/2020.

FACT FILE

Scientific name: *Macropus dorsalis*
Other name: Scrub wallaby
Colour: Brown and reddish fur, white front, black stripe from the head and down the back, with black paws
Size: Body about 80 centimetres long, plus tail
Habitat: Forests of eastern Australia
Food: Grasses and shrubs

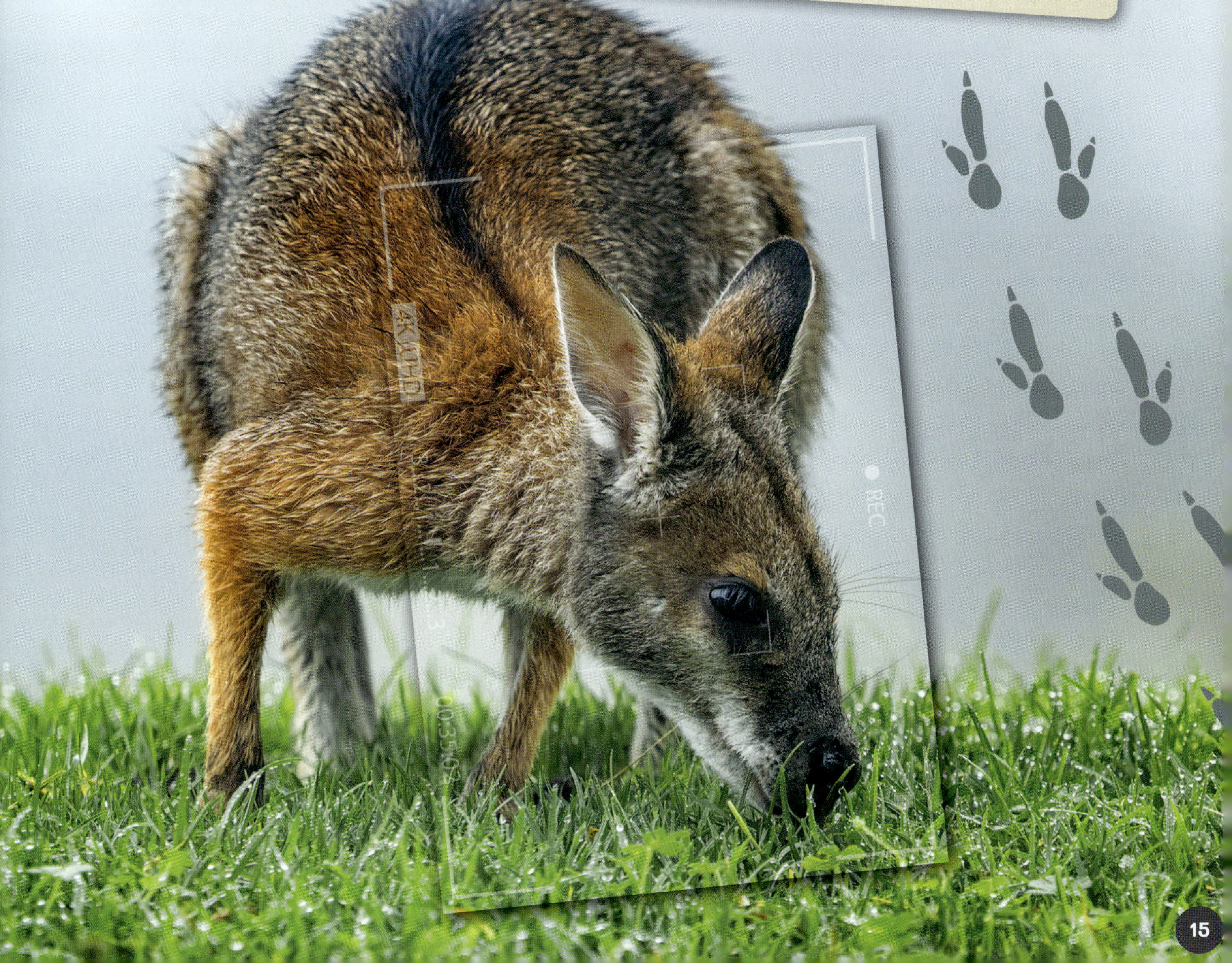

MALA

FACT FILE

Scientific name: *Lagorchestes hirsutus*
Other names: Rufous hare-wallaby
Colour: Pale grey with a white belly
Size: Body weighs about a kilogram, and is up to 40 centimetres long, plus tail
Habitat: Now only exists on islands off the Western Australian coast, where it lives amongst spinifex grasses, and in a few monitored areas on the mainland where it has been reintroduced
Food: Bushes and seeds

Close to extinction, the mala is a delightful little wallaby, with delicate back legs. They build burrows under spinifex plants, where they hide from the heat during the day.

TAMMAR WALLABY

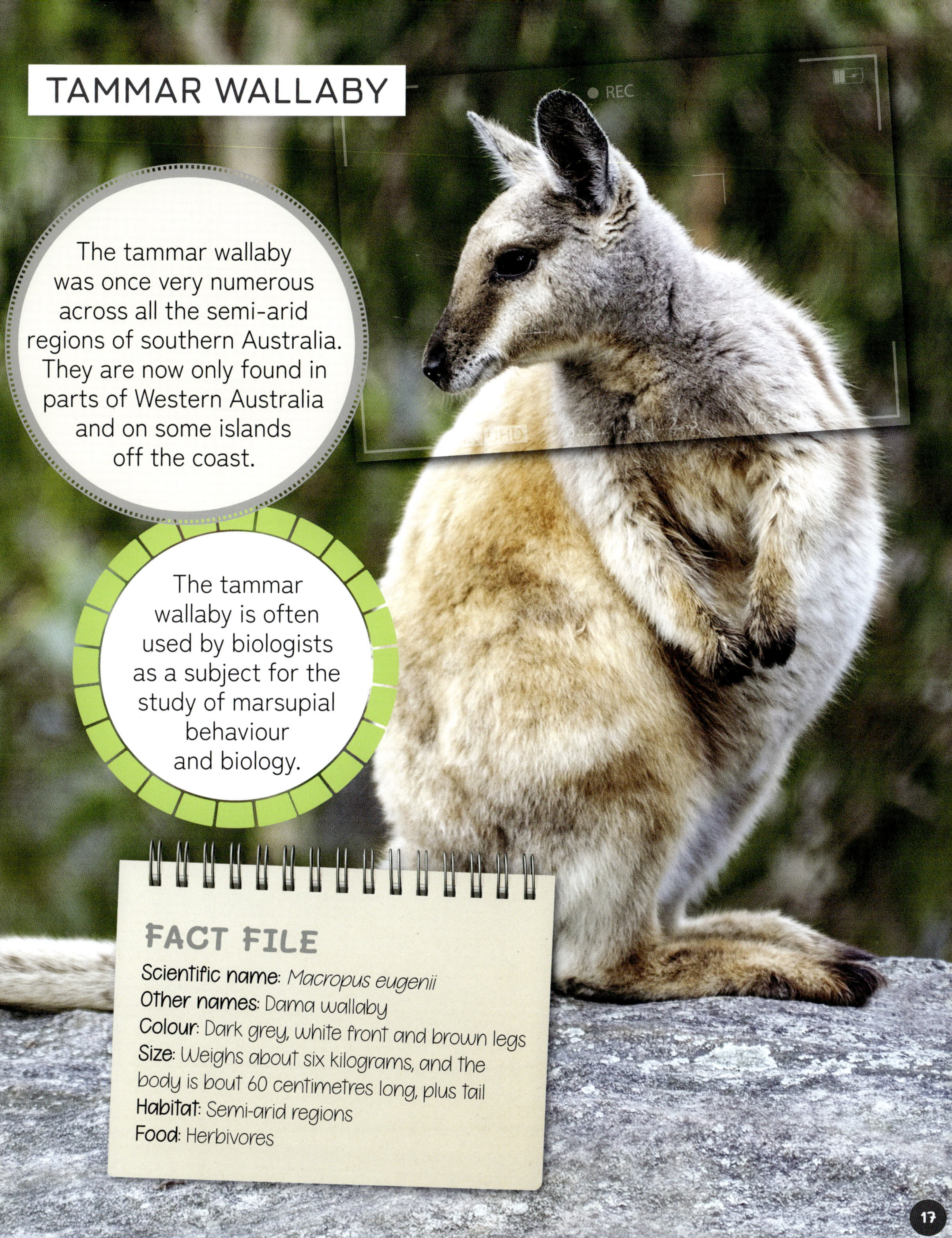

The tammar wallaby was once very numerous across all the semi-arid regions of southern Australia. They are now only found in parts of Western Australia and on some islands off the coast.

The tammar wallaby is often used by biologists as a subject for the study of marsupial behaviour and biology.

FACT FILE

Scientific name: *Macropus eugenii*
Other names: Dama wallaby
Colour: Dark grey, white front and brown legs
Size: Weighs about six kilograms, and the body is bout 60 centimetres long, plus tail
Habitat: Semi-arid regions
Food: Herbivores

PADEMELONS

FACT FILE

Scientific name: Genus *Thylogale*
Colour: Most have thick, grey or brown fur
Size: Up to a metre long, and weighing up to about six kilograms
Habitat: Forests and rainforests of eastern Australia and parts of New Guinea
Food: Herbivores

The pademelon is a small wallaby, with a little head, short tail, and a stocky, rounded body. In the colonial era of Australia, settlers hunted them for their meat.

Tasmanian devils, eagles and feral animals hunt the pademelons in Tasmania, with the young being particularly vulnerable to attack.

THE 3 SPECIES OF PADEMELON IN AUSTRALIA

- Red-necked pademelon
- Red-legged pademelon
- Tasmanian pademelon

WHIPTAIL WALLABY

This elegant animal deserves its nickname of pretty-faced wallaby. It has a long, whip-like tail and large ears.

FACT FILE

Scientific name: *Macropus parryi*
Other names: Pretty-faced wallaby
Colour: Light grey, with white cheeks, dark face, large eyes and thick eyelashes
Size: Weighs up to 20 kilograms and stands about a metre tall
Habitat: Forests and grasslands of eastern Australia
Food: Grazes on grass and small shrubs. Mobs of fifty whiptail wallabies often gather when feeding

Human hunters used to kill the whiptail wallaby to make its long tail into a leather whip.

WALLABY LIFE CYCLE

MARSUPIALS

Since all wallabies are marsupials, they have a different life cycle from placental mammals, such as cats and dogs. After mating, the female wallaby gives birth to a tiny baby that looks like an embryo. Instead of growing inside the mother, the baby crawls to a pouch or fold of skin on the outside of the mother's belly. It attaches itself to a nipple and starts to drink milk.

MOBS

A group of kangaroos or wallabies is called a mob. Although kangaroos may gather in huge mobs, wallabies tend to gather in smaller groups, or live mostly solitary lives.

LIFESPAN

The larger the wallaby, the longer its lifespan is. A large, red-necked wallaby can live for fifteen years, but a little rock wallaby might only live for two or three years in the wild.

JOEYS

Baby marsupials are called joeys. As they grow, they sometimes jump out of the mother's pouch to explore what is around, and then jump back in to sleep, drink and feel safe. When they are old enough to look after themselves, the joey leaves the mother and moves away to find its own area to live in.

WALLABY ANCESTORS

Macropods, including kangaroos, wallabies and wallaroos, are all descendants of the same ancient creatures that lived millions of years ago in Australia's rainforests. Since then, macropods evolved to have all the differences that we see today.

Prehistoric giant short-faced kangaroo

Allied rock wallaby

Wallaby mother and baby

Fossils of a giant wallaby called Protemnodon reveal that it was living in Australia from about five million years ago up until only 50,000 years ago. It weighed over 150 kilograms (that's as heavy as a panda bear!) and was one of a group of gigantic Australian animals called megafauna.

Illustration of banded hare-wallabies on Bernier Island

The little banded hare-wallaby (*Lagostrophus fasciatus*) may be a surprising, modern relative of the prehistoric, giant short-faced kangaroo (*Simosthenurus occidentalis*).

THREATS TO WALLABIES

IUCN RED LIST

The Red List is an international compilation of the conservation status of living things. Some wallabies are listed as being on the verge of extinction; others have become extinct only recently, but some have stable numbers and are not under threat of extinction.

HABITAT LOSS

Wallabies live in forests, bushland and rocky areas. The loss of their habitat and food sources is the major threat to their existence.

4K UHD 3..2..1..1..2...3 00:35:02

PREDATORS

Native predators include dingoes and eagles, with the young being particularly vulnerable. Feral dogs and cats also pose a threat to wallabies.

PROTECTING THEMSELVES

Wallabies are not well-equipped with weapons to defend themselves against predators. They do have large claws on their feet, but their small size makes them easy targets for canine predators.

WALLABIES AND PEOPLE

KEEPING A WALLABY

Small wallabies are very cute animals but taking them from the wild is against the law in Australia. No wallaby can be kept as a pet, and even wildlife careers need special permission to look after injured wallabies. As with any wild animal, wallabies can become very sick very quickly if they are not in their natural habitat and eating food from the wild.

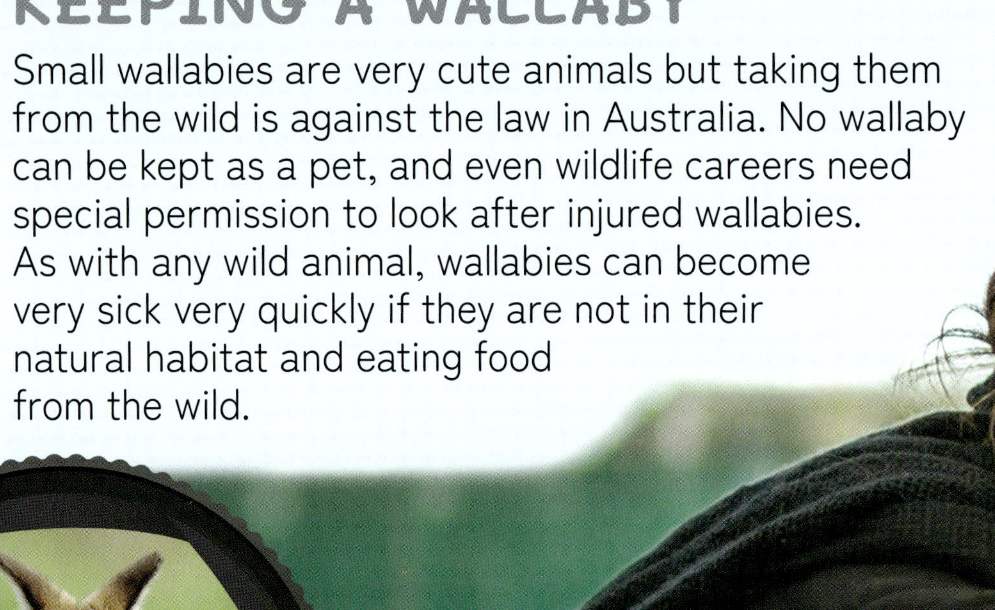

ZOOS

Zoos are the best places to see a wallaby up close. Some zoos have 'petting areas' where visitors can get very close to tame wallabies, and feed and pat them. A wild wallaby may scratch and bite if you try to get too near to it.

HUNTING

Before colonisation, wallabies were a food source for the Indigenous people of Australia. After 1788, colonists also hunted kangaroos and wallabies, but to such an extent that the numbers of many of the species were dramatically reduced. The introduction of dogs and foxes, and the destruction of natural habitats, were a major factor in the decline of many wallaby populations.

First Nations people used fire to hunt wildlife

ROADS

A dead wallaby beside a road is a sad reminder that wildlife and cars do not mix. A wallaby will often run across the path of a car, instead of away from it. This is a tactic that it uses to confuse a predator, but it does not work with a fast car.

SORTING ANIMALS INTO GROUPS

Biologists divide all living things around the world into groups. They call this process classification.

The two basic groups of animals are called:

VERTEBRATES

Vertebrates have a backbone

INVERTEBRATES

Invertebrates do not have a backbone

Vertebrates are further divided into groups shown below (classes). Wallabies are mammals and belong in the class called Mammalia.

MORE WALLABIES

Bridled nail-tail wallaby
Onychogalea fraenata

Red-legged pademelon
Thylogale stigmatica

Eastern hare-wallaby
Lagorchestes leporides

Western brush wallaby
Macropus irma

Yellow-footed rock-wallaby
Petrogale xanthopus
Tasmanian pademelon
Thylogale billardierii
Spectacled hare-wallaby
Lagorchestes conspicillatus
Brush-tailed rock-wallaby
Petrogale penicillata
00:35:02

GLOSSARY

adaptation change in a living thing to make it better able to survive

feral animal animals not native to an area

genetic diversity having a wide range of genes, leading to better chances of overcoming new diseases

joey baby marsupial

macropod marsupial with large feet

marsupial mammal group that produces underdeveloped babies that drink milk from the mother

mob group of macropods

solitary being alone

spinifex spiky grass that grows in semi-arid parts of Australia

tactic plan for doing something

vulnerable easily harmed

INDEX